Raves for Terrence McNally and
Master Class

"Funny and moving. . . . An homage to teaching as well as to Maria Callas, Terrence McNally's beautiful new play is set at Juilliard during one of La Divina's famous master classes." —*Variety*

"Howlingly funny and uncommonly perceptive about the irrational entertainment we call opera. . . . Resounds with the ring of truth." —*San Francisco Examiner*

"Marvelous . . . elegant simplicity." —*LA Weekly*

"Spectacular . . . an inspired work . . . passionately written." —*New York Law Journal*

"An arresting impression of a troubled artist consumed by the quest for truth and tortured by her own frailties." —*Los Angeles Times*

Terrence McNally is the author of numerous plays, including *Love! Valour! Compassion!* (winner of the Tony Award for best play), *The Ritz,* and *Frankie and Johnny in the Claire de Lune,* which was made into a feature film starring Al Pacino and Michelle Pfeiffer, and the books for the musicals *The Rink* and *Kiss of the Spider Woman* (winner of the Tony Award for the best book of a musical). Other successes include *Lips Together, Teeth Apart* and *The Lisbon Traviata.* McNally has received two Guggenheim Fellowships, a Rockefeller Grant, and a citation from the American Academy of Arts and Letters. He also serves as vice president for the Dramatists Guild, the national organization of playwrights, composers, and lyricists. He lives in New York City.

Master Class

TERRENCE McNALLY

Master Class

A PLUME BOOK

PLUME
Published by the Penguin Group
Penguin Books USA Inc., 375 Hudson Street,
New York, New York 10014, U.S.A.
Penguin Books Ltd, 27 Wrights Lane,
London W8 5TZ, England
Penguin Books Australia Ltd, Ringwood,
Victoria, Australia
Penguin Books Canada Ltd, 10 Alcorn Avenue,
Toronto, Ontario, Canada M4V 3B2
Penguin Books (N.Z.) Ltd, 182–190 Wairau Road,
Auckland 10, New Zealand

Penguin Books Ltd, Registered Offices:
Harmondsworth, Middlesex, England

First published by Plume, an imprint of Dutton Signet,
a division of Penguin Books USA Inc.

℗ REGISTERED TRADEMARK—MARCA REGISTRADA

ISBN 0-452-27615-2

Printed in the United States of America
Set in Times Roman and Gill Sans Light

For Elaine Steinbeck
Fanciulla del West

Master Class was first produced by the Philadelphia Theatre Company at the Plays and Players Theatre on March 1, 1995. Subsequently, the production traveled to the Mark Taper Forum in Los Angeles, the Eisenhower Theatre at the Kennedy Center in Washington, D.C., and the Golden Theatre in New York City where it opened on November 5, 1995, and was produced by Robert Whitehead, Lewis Allen and Spring Sorkin.

CAST

MARIA	Zoe Caldwell
FIRST SOPRANO (Sophie)	Karen Kay Cody
SECOND SOPRANO (Sharon)	Audra McDonald
TENOR (Tony)	Jay Hunter Morris
ACCOMPANIST (Manny)	David Loud
STAGEHAND	Michael Friel

The production was directed by Leonard Foglia. The set designer was Michael McGarty. The lighting designer was Brian MacDevitt. The costume designer was Jane Greenwood. The production stage manager was Dianne Trulock. The stage manager was Linda Barnes. The assistant to Mr. McNally and Mr. Foglia was Thomas Caruso.

The playwright wishes to acknowledge the crucial role The Gathering at Big Fork, Montana, played in the development of his script. Zoe Caldwell, Leonard Foglia and Karen Kay Cody took part when the play was first read there in the spring of 1994.

ACT ONE

The house lights are still up when the ACCOMPANIST *takes his place at the piano. He adjusts his seat. He checks his music. He waves at friends in the audience—if he has any.*

MARIA *enters. She is dressed in an expensive pants suit, accessorized with an Hermès scarf. She wears expensive Italian shoes and carries a largish Chanel bag. She walks briskly to the stage apron.*

MARIA: No applause. We're here to work. You're not in a theatre. This is a classroom. No folderol. This is a master class. Singing is serious business. We're going to roll up our sleeves and work. I appreciate your welcome, but enough is enough. *Basta. Fini.* Eh?

So. How is everyone? Can you hear me? I don't believe in microphones. Singing is first of all about projection. So is speech. People are forgetting how to listen. They want everything blasted at them. Listening takes concentration. If you can't hear me, it's your fault. You're not concentrating. I don't get any louder than this. So come down closer or leave. No takers? What? You're all scared of me? Eh? Is that it? I don't bite. I promise you. I bark —I bark quite a bit actually—but I don't bite. I don't know what you're expecting. What did they tell you? I hope you're not expecting me to sing. Well, we shall see what we shall see.

Allora, so, let's begin. Where is the first student? Who is the first student? Are they here? When I was a student, I never missed a lesson. Never. Not once. I was never late for one either. In fact, I was usually early. I never wanted to leave the conservatory. I lived, ate, and slept music. Music is a discipline. Too many of you are looking for the easy way out. Short cuts. No. If you want to have a career, as I did—and I'm not boasting now, I am not one to boast—you must be willing to subjugate yourself—is that a word?—subjugate yourself to the music. Always the music. You are its servant. You are here to serve the composer. The composer is God. In Athens, and this was during the war, I often went to bed hungry, but I walked to the conservatory and back every day, six days a week, and sometimes my feet were bleeding because I had no proper shoes. I don't tell you this to melodramatize. Oh no. I tell you to show you who I am. Discipline. Courage. Here. Right here. From the guts.

These lights. Who is in charge of these lights? Is someone in charge of these lights? May we have the lights in the auditorium off, please? This is really terrible. We can't work under these conditions. I'm not going to ask a student to come out here until these lights are taken care of. This is what I was talking about. Attention must be paid to every detail. The lights. Your wig. The amount of stage dust. A career in the theatre demands total concentration. One hundred percent detail. You think I'm joking? I'm not joking. You wait, you'll see. If you're ever so lucky to sing in one of the great theatres. I mean La Scala. I mean Covent Garden. I mean l'Opéra. I mean Vienna. I mean the Metropolitan. You think it's easy? A great career? Ha! That's all I have to say to you. Ha! Is this my

water here? And is this my chair? I don't see a cushion.
I asked for a cushion. Thank you.
  (*To the* ACCOMPANIST:) Hello. You don't look fa-
miliar. Have I seen you before? Where? When? Speak up,
I can't hear you if you mumble.

ACCOMPANIST: We worked on *Don Carlo.*

MARIA: I can't hear him. Can you hear him? No one can hear
you.

ACCOMPANIST: Yesterday morning, we worked on *Don Carlo*
together. Eboli's aria, "O don fatale."

MARIA: Was that you? You look different. You were wearing
a red sweater. Where is it? It's important to have a look.
A signature. Be someone. So people will remember you.
You all think you're so special. You're a dime a dozen.
There are hundreds, no, thousands of you out there, study-
ing, auditioning, going here, there, hither and yon. You
expect people to remember you if you don't have a look?
Po, po, po! I was never arrogant that way. I knew I needed
a look and I got one.
  You. Yes, you. And don't take this personally. You
don't have a look. You look very nice, I'm sure you are.
You look very clean, very *comme il faut*, but you don't
have a look. Get one. As quickly as possible. It's much
easier than practicing your scales. Or maybe it's not. When
you weigh five hundred kilos—like some singers I could
mention but I won't—a look is a little more difficult. What
are you smirking about? Yes, you, right behind this person
without a look. You don't have a look either. In fact, I
don't see anyone out there with what I consider a look. If
you do, and I haven't seen you, and I don't have the best
vision in the world (we'll speak more about that later!), if
you do, I salute you. If you don't, get one.

(The house lights are turned down.)

There. *Bravo!* Now we have the atmosphere for some serious work. Isn't that much better? Thank you. I said, no applause. This is not a circus. I really must insist. All it takes is one troublemaker to spoil the concentration. You are here to observe the students. Not me. Forget all about me. Poof! I'm invisible.

(*To the* ACCOMPANIST:) What's your name?

ACCOMPANIST: Me?

MARIA: Unless you want me to refer to you as "The Person Who Was Wearing A Red Sweater Yesterday Morning."

ACCOMPANIST: Manny.

MARIA: Manny?

ACCOMPANIST: Short for Emmanuel.

MARIA: Emmanuel. That's a Jewish name, I would imagine.

ACCOMPANIST: Yes.

MARIA: And you are Jewish.

ACCOMPANIST: Yes.

MARIA: I don't think there's a person in this auditorium who doesn't know that Eboli's aria is "O don fatale." Eh? So. Your little . . . how shall we say . . . dig? reminder? . . . was quite unnecessary. Have I made myself clear? Eh?

ACCOMPANIST: Yes. I only.

MARIA: I accept your apology. How was I?

ACCOMPANIST: Pardon?

MARIA: When we worked on the *Don Carlo,* how was I? Don't answer that. This isn't about me.

Now. Our first victim. Where is she?

ACCOMPANIST: You were wonderful.

MARIA: Thank you. It's a glorious bit of music. But really, you shouldn't have said that. This isn't about me. I'm quite cross with you, Manny. Is it all right if I call you Manny?

ACCOMPANIST: Please, I insist.

MARIA: And you must call me Madame. That was a little joke. So was "victim." Sooner or later you'll catch on to my sense of humor. Or you won't. Some people don't think I have one. Tenors. See? I can be witty. Only let's get down to the serious business at hand. We'll save the jokes for out there. The real world. Whatever that means. Brutal expression. Brutal place. At least in here we know where we are. We know where we stand. *Allora.* Is it me or is it warm in here? Can someone do something about the temperature? I won't have my singers sweating like pigs. It's hard enough supporting a tone with our diaphragms without dealing with overheating. Of course in Athens during the war there was no heat at all, but that's another story. We froze, but did we complain? Not a word. We were just grateful to be alive. Elvira de Hidalgo, a great soprano and my only teacher, Madame de Hidalgo used to say to me, "Maria, I have never seen anyone suffer so much in silence." Be that as it may. I guess I was made of sterner stuff. I had to be. Well, that and twenty-five cents will get you a token on the subway. I believe that's your expression for it. Nobody cares the troubles you've seen. It's our work that matters. Only our work.

Well. I'm ready. Are you? Has the heat been taken care of? I might as well be talking to myself.

ACCOMPANIST: They're working on it.

MARIA: And I am the Grand Duchess Anastasia Romanoff and the check is in the mail. Is the first singer ready? Don't just stand there. *Avanti*, darling, *avanti*.

(*The* SOPRANO *comes onto the stage.*)

We'll be right with you.

And while you're fixing the heat and getting the cushion I requested at least three times before coming out here, the last being only an hour ago, would you see if you could find a little footrest for me? You see, my feet aren't going to quite reach the ground when I sit in such an uncommonly high chair as the one you've provided me with. Thank you. I'm sure that's the last we'll see of those people! *Coraggio.*

(*To the* SOPRANO:) I'm sorry.

SOPRANO: That's all right.

MARIA: Close your ears, child. You're just what I was talking about. I said, close your ears. I don't want you to hear this. Are they closed?

SOPRANO: Yes.

MARIA: This is just what I was talking about. She doesn't have a look, poor thing. I'm not talking about her face, her figure. She can't help them. I'm talking about flair, style, élan. Even the most wretched of us can do something about them. All right, you can open them. Did you hear that?

SOPRANO: No.

MARIA: Good. Well, hello, welcome. Are you nervous?

SOPRANO: Yes, a little.

MARIA: Only a little? You should be nervous a lot! All these people looking at you, waiting to hear what you sound like, all ready to judge you? I'd be terrified.

SOPRANO: I am, I am.

MARIA: Well stop it. You can't sing if you're nervous. You can't do anything if you're nervous. Nerves have destroyed more singers than a bad teacher ever did. All nerves mean is a lack of confidence. A lack of preparation. Do I make you nervous?

SOPRANO: Yes.

MARIA: Good. I take this seriously and so should you.

SOPRANO: I do.

MARIA: Eh?

SOPRANO: I do take this seriously.

MARIA: What's your name? Eh? You'll have to speak up, darling. You're on a stage now. People are listening. Hundreds and hundreds of people. They want to know who you are. Don't disappoint them. God gave you a voice. Use it.

SOPRANO: Sophie De Palma.

MARIA: *Brava!* See how easy that was! Sophie De Palma. It's not an ideal name for a career, but it's good enough. I can see it outside a theatre: Sophie De Palma as . . . what? Sophie De Palma as Frasquita in *Carmen.* Sophie De Palma as the Third Norn in *Götterdämmerung.* Italian?

SOPRANO: Greek/Italian.

MARIA: *Po, po, po!*

SOPRANO: My teacher says that accounts for my temperament. I'm very fiery.

MARIA: Are you?

SOPRANO: That's what my teacher says. I was making a little joke. I don't believe you can be a great artist without temperament. Neither does she. We're working on it. Everyone said you had, I mean have, great temperament. I'm hoping to get some from you, frankly. Am I saying the wrong thing?

MARIA: Do something fiery.

SOPRANO: I can't. Not just like that. No one can.

MARIA: WHERE IS MY FOOTSTOOL?

SOPRANO: Well, I guess some people can.

MARIA: You thought that was fiery? Wait. Just wait. My fire comes from here, Sophie. It's mine. It's not for sale. It's not for me to give away. And even if I could, I wouldn't. It's who I am. Find out who you are. That's what this is all about. Eh? This isn't a freak show. I'm not a performing seal. "I'm hoping to get some from you, frankly"!

SOPRANO: I'm sorry.

MARIA: So. What are you going to sing for us? Sophie De Palma?

SOPRANO: *Sonnambula*? "Ah, non credea mirarti."

MARIA: *Brava!*

SOPRANO: Is that all right?

MARIA: Into the lion's den, eh? I salute your courage. Be our guest. One of the most beautiful bel canto arias, if not the most difficult.

SOPRANO: They say you were unsurpassed in the role. I have your recording, of course. Even Sutherland.

MARIA: Stop right there. This is important. For all of us. I won't hear anything against any of my colleagues. And neither should you. She did her best. That's all any of us can do. Joan was. Well, that's a whole other story. But she did her best. Like her looks, it wasn't her fault. A twelve-foot Lucia di Lammermoor. Who ever heard of such a thing? But what was she to do? Stoop her way through the role? I don't want this class to disintegrate into a discussion of personalities. I won't let it happen.
   (*To the* ACCOMPANIST:) What?

ACCOMPANIST: Me?

MARIA: Yes, you. Who else? You've been trying to get a word in. I saw you back there. I have eyes in the back of my head. You have to if you want a career in the theatre. Someone somewhere is always behind you plotting your downfall. That's a fact. Always. If you don't develop eyes in the back of your head, you'll soon end up with a dagger in your back. Look what they did to me. The envy. The malice. But that's another story. So? What? Speak. We're wasting valuable time.

ACCOMPANIST: The footstool. It's here.

MARIA: Well, bring it out. Do I have to do everything myself? This is impossible.

ACCOMPANIST: They didn't want to interrupt.

MARIA: What would you call this? Do you understand now what I go through? All I'm trying to do is hold a simple master class.

(A STAGEHAND *brings out a footstool. He wears jeans and a T-shirt.*)

STAGEHAND: Where do you want it?

MARIA: There.

STAGEHAND: Here?

MARIA: That's where the chair is.

(*He puts the footstool down in front of* MARIA's *chair.*)

Bravo! Well done.

STAGEHAND: Hunh?

MARIA: See how simple that was? Tell your supervisor we can begin now. Thank you.

STAGEHAND: I don't have a supervisor. You're welcome.

(*He goes.*)

MARIA: People like that have absolutely no interest in what we're doing here. It's very humbling. We bare our hearts and they say "Hunh?" I always thought our art reached everyone. Well, I used to think a lot of things I don't anymore. Eh? So. Carmen De Palma? Are you ready? Straighten up. Head high. We're not hiding anything.

SOPRANO: It's Sophie. Sophie De Palma. You said Carmen.

MARIA: I can't be expected to keep everyone's name straight. I'm focused on the music now. And so should you be. Manny? Are you ready? Did I get that right at least? You are Manny?

ACCOMPANIST: Yes.

MARIA: Well, I'm good for something. I'm going to sit down now. Ignore me. Forget all about me. Poof! I'm invisible. I asked for a cushion, too. You see? You see? Never mind now. It's too late. We're working. All right. Now I want total silence and complete concentration. Sophie De Palma. Amina's aria. *La Sonnambula.* Good luck.

(*She makes herself comfortable.*)

You see why I asked for this stool? I have short legs. I always looked tall in the theatre, but I always had short legs. When Zeffirelli dressed me in *Norma.* But that's another story. Are you waiting for me? Begin.

(*The* ACCOMPANIST *begins to play.*)

Posture, posture. Not yours. Hers!

(*She listens to the introduction to the* scena *and recitative.*)

SOPRANO: "Oh!"

MARIA: Stop right there. I'm sorry to do this to you, but what's the point of going on with it if it's all wrong? Eh? You're not listening to the music.

SOPRANO: I wasn't?

MARIA: Let it fill you up. It's so simple. Listen. It's all there. Who she is. You don't have to do anything but listen. A simple country girl. An innocent victim. He's broken her heart. Have you ever had your heart broken?

SOPRANO: Yes.

MARIA: You could have fooled me. This is the theatre, darling. We wear our hearts on our sleeves here.

SOPRANO: But she's sleepwalking. She's a sleepwalker.

MARIA: She's not a sleepwalker. That's the artifice. Something some writer made up so there could be a silly story. Find the truth of her situation. A broken heart. Anyone can walk in their sleep. Very few people can weep in song. Again, Manny. I'm sorry to interrupt so quickly before you've

scarcely sung a note, but I get so impatient when I see a
singer who doesn't listen to the music. I'll be very good
this time. I promise.

(*The* ACCOMPANIST *begins to play again.*)

Better, better. You're listening. I'm seeing Bellini on your
face. *Attenzione!* Now I'm seeing terror. Now I'm seeing
Sophie. Do you mind if I do it?

SOPRANO: Please. I wish you would.

MARIA: I don't want you to imitate me. I never want any of
you to imitate me. I only want to show you how I did it.
It's so hard to say what I mean. So much easier to show
you. All right, now at La Scala when I worked with Luchino, Visconti, Luchino Visconti, the *régisseur*, the *met-
teur en scene*, you know him in this country, eh? Luchino
had me appear high above the stage. One false step and I
would have fallen to my death. A fate that would not have
distressed some of my colleagues who were sitting out
front. Colleagues? Enemies, I should say. So. There I am.
Sleepwalking. My heart broken. Unaware that death is but
one false step away. I'm ready.

(*She nods to the* ACCOMPANIST. *He plays the introduction.*
MARIA *stands and listens to its end, then:*)

Well, something like that. No applause.

SOPRANO: That was wonderful.

MARIA: See how easy that was?

SOPRANO: I'll try.

MARIA: Just listen. Everything is in the music.

(*She listens as the* ACCOMPANIST *plays again.*)

SOPRANO: "Oh!"

MARIA: You know I'm going to interrupt you again, don't you?

SOPRANO: Yes. But I was listening that time, wasn't I? I really thought I was listening.

MARIA: You can listen till the cows come home. Is that the expression? Listening is beyond the point. We're singing now. I want to talk about your "Oh!"

SOPRANO: I sang it, didn't I?

MARIA: That's just it. You sang it. You didn't feel it. It's not a note we're after here. It's a stab of pain. The pain of loss. Surely you understand loss. If not another person, then maybe a pet. A puppy. A goldfish. It's not a question of singing. Anyone can get the notes out. Well, that's not true, actually Scotto had no business singing this music. Know your limitations. That's important. So, what are we talking about here, eh? Feeling, feeling, feeling. "Oh!" You hear the difference?

SOPRANO: Yes.

MARIA: I want to hear everything in that one sound. "Oh!" Can you give me that?

SOPRANO: I'll try.

MARIA: Try isn't good enough. *Do.* The theatre isn't about trying. People don't leave their homes to watch us try. They come to see us do.

All right, you can come out now. Excuse me, Sophie.

(*The* STAGEHAND *appears with a cushion for* MARIA.)

Avanti, avanti! The theatre isn't for people who like to be in their ivory towers either.

STAGEHAND: Is this what you wanted?

MARIA: It's fine. Interruptions every moment.

STAGEHAND: You said you wanted this.

MARIA: I did. This is a class. I'm making a point. You're singing an aria and they're building scenery in the wings.

STAGEHAND: I wasn't building any scenery.

MARIA: You see? You see?

STAGEHAND: Anything else?

MARIA: No. Let's give him a hand. (*Watching him go:*) Couldn't care less! *Allora.* Where were we? Ah, yes, "Oh!" I'm not going to stop you this time, *cara.* Now, I may speak to you while you sing, but I'm not going to stop you.

ACCOMPANIST: Again?

MARIA: If you please. Posture.

(*The* ACCOMPANIST *begins again. The* SOPRANO *begins again. This time* MARIA *looks for something in her purse while the* ACCOMPANIST *and the* SOPRANO *continue.*)

Go ahead. I'm listening. There it is! I thought I'd lost it. Continue.

SOPRANO: "Oh! se una volta sola"

MARIA: Diction, diction! "Volta." Bite into those consonants. I want to hear them. There's an *l* in "volta," there's a *t.*

SOPRANO: "volta sola,
         Rivederlo io potessi"

MARIA: "Rivederlo"! Where's your *r* in "rivederlo"?

SOPRANO: "Rivederlo io potessi,
         Anzi che all'ara altra sposa
         Ei guidasse! . . ."

Zoe Caldwell as Maria Callas.

Photos of the original cast by Joan Marcus.

Karen Kay Cody as Sophie *(left)* with David Loud as Manny *(center)* and Zoe Caldwell as Callas.

Jay Hunter Morris as Tony *(right)* with David Loud as Manny *(center)* and Zoe Caldwell as Callas.

Audra McDonald as Sharon with Zoe Caldwell as Callas.

MARIA: I'm not hearing any consonants. You're singing in Sanskrit. I'm only getting vowels. Words mean something. Vowels are the inarticulate sounds our hearts make. "Oh." Consonants give them specific meaning. "Oh! se una volta sola." Hear the difference? "Volta sola." Does that make any sense? Eh? I just made that up. Vowels, consonants. But I think I'm on to something. Eh? You. I like you. You nod and smile at everything I say. (*To the* SOPRANO:) What are you saying?

SOPRANO: You mean.

MARIA: The words.

SOPRANO: I'm saying.

MARIA: Translate them.

SOPRANO: "Oh!" Obviously, "Oh!" means "Oh!" If one time alone. Or more. If one more time. See him again, I could. No, wait. "If only I could see him one more time again." Something like that.

MARIA: Hmmmmmm.

SOPRANO: If only one more time I could see him again.

MARIA: May I?

ACCOMPANIST: From the top?

MARIA: Yes. From the top. This is music, not piecework.

(*She nods to the* ACCOMPANIST, *who plays the introduction as* MARIA *speaks the words.*)

"Oh! se una volta sola"—hear the difference? "Volta sola. Rivederlo io potessi." She's never going to see this man again. "Anzi che all'ara altra sposa ei guidasse!" "Before he takes another bride to the altar." "Vana speranza." What a terrible expression—"vain hope." Her life is over. "Io sento suonar la sacra squilla." She hears the wedding bells. They don't ring for her. "Al tempio ei muove"—"They're on their way to the church"! "Io l'ho perduto"—"I've lost him." "E pur"—this is important—"E pur"—"and yet, and yet"—"rea non son io." "I am not guilty." I wasn't.

SOPRANO: This is hard.

MARIA: Of course it's hard. That's why it's so important we do it right. "This is hard." Where am I? I thought I was somewhere where people were serious. This is not a film studio where anyone can get up there and act. I hate that word. "Act." No! Feel. Be. That's what we're doing here. "This is hard." I'll tell you what's hard. What's hard is listening to you make a mockery of this work of art. "Mockery" is too strong a word. So is "travesty." I'm not getting any juice from you, Sophie. I want juice. I want passion. I want you.

SOPRANO: I'm not that sort of singer.

MARIA: Well try. Just once in your life, try.

SOPRANO: I'm not that sort of person either.

MARIA: What sort of person are you then?

SOPRANO: I just want to sing.

MARIA: Am I stopping you?

SOPRANO: No. You're.

MARIA: We don't have to finish this. If you're unhappy.

SOPRANO: I don't know what you're talking about.

MARIA: Yes, you do. You just don't want to do it. Everyone understood what I was talking about when I was singing. They simply didn't want to listen. Too difficult. Too painful. Too controversial. I don't blame them. I did but I don't now. Why deal with someone like me when you can have Tebaldi or Sutherland or Sills? They said they didn't like my sound. That wasn't it. They didn't like my soul. Too. What? Too. Something. You have a lovely voice, you know. A charming sound.

SOPRANO: Thank you.

MARIA: Much lovelier than mine ever was. And no one ever accused me or my voice of charm. That was my sister. She was the charming one. The pretty one. The one the boys. Wanted. Anyway. *En tout cas.* All that got her, wherever she is—I don't know, we don't speak—and got me, where I am—sometimes I think the whole world knows where that is, or was, and which is right now up here with you talking to you about your voice, your sound. Who you are. Who are you? Sophie De Palma—you've told us your name, but who are you? Tears will get you nowhere, darling. Not in the theatre, not in real life. Certainly not with me. No one cares how many nights I cried myself to sleep. I sang Norma better than anyone had in years and I interpolated a high F at the end of the first act. That's all people cared about. When you're fat and ugly (and I'm not saying that you are either of those things) you had better have a couple of high F's you can inter-polate into your life. No one cares about your damp pil-low. Why should I? Did you care about mine? Did anyone? But that's another story. I can cry all I want now (don't worry, I won't; tears come hard when you're me) but you can't, Sophie De Palma. You've got to sing for your supper. Sing for your salvation. Shall we try again?

(*The* SOPRANO *nods.* MARIA *gives her a tissue and glances at her watch.*)

Did you know one of my baptismal Greek Orthodox names was Sophie?

SOPRANO: No.

MARIA: Cecilia Sophia Anna Maria Kalogeropoulou. December 2, 19. But that was in another life. *Allora. Cominciamo. Ricominciamo.*

SOPRANO: From "Gran Dio"?

MARIA: *Va bene.*
    If you're not enjoying this, you can leave. No one's keeping you.
    We have someone going through his diary in the third row, Sophie. I told him if he wasn't enjoying our work here, he's free to leave.
    Are we ready?

(*The* SOPRANO *and the* ACCOMPANIST *nod.*)

Do you call them that in this country? Diaries? Agendas? Never mind. Sshh! Before we start, what is the orchestra playing here, darling?

SOPRANO: Nothing?

MARIA: And why do you think that is? What is Bellini up to?

SOPRANO: I don't know.

MARIA: He wants us to concentrate on the sound of the human voice. The most expressive instrument there is to reveal human emotion. Bellini wants us to hear you in all your glory in the *recitativo*. When you can no longer bear to speak, when the words aren't enough, that's when he asks you to sing. Not a moment before.

SOPRANO: But recitative is singing, surely.

MARIA: Of course it's singing. It's sung. But it's the equivalent of speech. Eh? Again.

SOPRANO: Again? I haven't. Once. I'm sorry.

MARIA: Remember to use the words. From "Gran Dio."

SOPRANO (*singing*): "Gran Dio."

MARIA: What are you doing?

SOPRANO: I'm sorry?

MARIA: What does it say in the score?

SOPRANO: I begin on the C above middle C and.

MARIA: I'm not talking about notes. There's a direction from the composer.

SOPRANO: There is?

(*The* SOPRANO *goes to piano and looks at music the* ACCOMPANIST *is playing from.*)

MARIA: This is what I've been talking about the entire time. This lack of detail. This sense of nothing matters.

SOPRANO: You mean "inginocchiandosi"? (*She has difficulty with the word.*)

MARIA: I mean "inginocchiandosi." (*She doesn't.*)

SOPRANO: It's important?

MARIA: It's life and death, like everything we do here.

SOPRANO: I don't know what it means.

MARIA: We can see that.

SOPRANO: It's a reflexive verb, I know that much. It means I do something to myself.

MARIA: Don't tempt me to tell you what that might be. Kneel.

SOPRANO: Kneel?

MARIA: It means "kneel." *Così!*

(*She drops to her knees and opens her arms wide.*)

"Gran Dio!" This is how we speak to God. On our knees, *a terra*, our arms open to Him. "Non mirar il mio pianto." "Do not heed these tears I shed." "Io gliel perdono." "I forgive him them." The orchestra is sounding like an organ here. A church organ. What is Bellini up to? "Quanto infelice io sono, felice ei sia." "Let him be as happy as I am unhappy." "Questa d'un cor che muore è l'ultima preghiera." "This is the last prayer of a heart that is dying." That explains the organ. It's all in the music. "Ah, sì!" She says it again. She has to. "Questa d'un cor che muore è l'ultima preghiera."

SOPRANO: I see what you mean now.

MARIA: What do you do now? What does the score say?

SOPRANO (*haltingly*): "Guardandosi la mano—"

MARIA: "Guardandosi la mano come cercando l'anello."

(*She looks at her left hand for a ring that isn't there.*)

"L'anello mio."

SOPRANO: "My ring"!

MARIA: "L'anello."

SOPRANO: "The ring."

MARIA: "Ei me l'ha tolto."

SOPRANO: "He took it from me."

MARIA: "Ma non può rapirmi l'immagin sua . . ."

SOPRANO: But he cannot from me take image his. His image.

MARIA: "Sculta ella è qui . . ."

SOPRANO: "Sculptured it is here."

MARIA: "Here!" "Qui . . . nel petto."

(MARIA *takes flowers from her bosom as the* SOPRANO *reads from the score.*)

SOPRANO: "Amina takes Elvino's faded flowers from her bosom."

(*She stops and watches* MARIA.)

MARIA (*spoken*):

"Ah! non credea mirarti
Sì presto estinto, o fiore,
Passasti al par d'amore,
Che un giorno solo, che un giorno sol durò.
Che un giorno solo, ah, sol durò.

"Potria novel vigore
Il pianto, il pianto mio recarti . . .
Ma ravvivar l'amore
Il pianto mio, ah no, no, non può
Ah, non credea
Passasti al par d'amor, d'amor, ecc."

(*She continues to end of the aria.*)

No applause.
Something like that, Sophie. Eh?
You see what I mean now?

SOPRANO: I think so. Thank you.

MARIA: You think you can do that?

SOPRANO: I'll. Yes.

MARIA: Did you mark your score? Those phrases I pointed out?

SOPRANO: No.

MARIA: Why not?

SOPRANO: I don't have a pencil.

MARIA: Then how do you expect to remember what you've learned? Five, maybe ten years from now, you'll be singing this role in some little theatre somewhere and you'll be saying to yourself, What did she tell me? What did she say? Does anyone have a pencil for a student who doesn't have one? If you can imagine such a thing.

SOPRANO: I didn't think we'd be.

ACCOMPANIST: I have one.

MARIA: Thank you.

SOPRANO: Thank you.

MARIA: At the conservatory Madame de Hidalgo never once had to ask me if I had a pencil. And this was during the war, when a pencil wasn't something you just picked up at the five and ten. Oh no, no, no, no. A pencil meant something. It was a choice over something else. You either had a pencil or an orange. I always had a pencil. I never had an orange. And I love oranges. I knew one day I would have all the oranges I could want, but that didn't make the wanting them any less.

    Have you ever been hungry?

SOPRANO: Not like that.

MARIA: It's. It's something you remember. Always. In some part of you.

You should see my scores. They're covered with pencil marks. You can hardly see the music. I wrote down everything. Every hint, every trick, every suggestion. Like a sponge I was. You have to be like a sponge. Absorb, absorb. These are centuries of opera we're talking about here, eh? We don't make this music up. The notes, the phrasing. We're talking about tradition.

Do you know who created Amina?

SOPRANO: You mean who.

MARIA: The same soprano who created Norma.

SOPRANO: They did?

MARIA: Pasta. Giuditta Pasta.

SOPRANO: I've heard of her.

MARIA: She'll be happy to hear that. When you sing this music I want to hear all the links that take you back to her. I want to hear Callas, I want to hear Milanov, I want to hear Ponselle, I want to hear Lehmann, I want to hear Pasta.

SOPRANO: Do you want to hear Sutherland? I'm sorry.

MARIA: I want to hear you. A straight line. From you through me to Pasta. Eh? How can you sing this music and not know who Pasta was? Shame, Sophie, shame.

SOPRANO: I know who Ponselle and Milanov are.

MARIA: Are we getting restless out there? I hear you getting restless. Stop it. This instant. We're working up here. Show some respect. I hate to say it, but you should wear longer skirts or slacks. During daytime it's all right. But you must remember, I'm sorry I'm bringing this up, but the public that looks at you from down there sees a little

more of you than you might want. Eh? It's no use now.
You should have thought of it before. Forgive me, eh? No
laughing. This is a serious matter. All right. Let's hear it
again. With a broken heart this time. Maestro.

(*The* ACCOMPANIST *begins to play again.*)

I'm not going to interrupt. Just listen. You're on your own.
In bocca al lupo. You know what that means?

SOPRANO: No.

MARIA: Good luck.

(*The* SOPRANO *begins the recitative again as lights fade on
her and* ACCOMPANIST *and come up strong on* MARIA, *who is
hearing her own performance of the same music. So are we.*)

How quickly it all comes back. The great nights.

(*She listens.*)

Ma, Luchino, perchè? Why do you have me wearing jew-
els? I am supposed to be a poor Swiss village girl. "You
are not a village girl. You are Maria Callas playing a village girl." Ah, capisco, capisco! I understood.

(*She listens.*)

This was the terrifying moment. The beginning. In the
utter, utter silence, my voice filling the void of that vast,
darkened auditorium. I felt so alone, so unprotected. *Coraggio.* It's begun.

(*She listens.*)

What were they expecting?

(*She listens.*)

Ari always said, They're not coming to hear you, no one
comes to hear Callas anymore. They've come to look at

you. You're not a singer. You're a freak. I'm a freak.
We're both freaks. They've come to see us. You're a mon-
stre sacré now. We are both monstres sacrés. And we are
fucking.
       I don't like that word, Ari.
       Fuck you, you don't like that word.

(*She listens.*)

       This phrase. Lovely. And I did it well.
       Did you hear what I said? Before you were just a
singer. A canary who sang for her supper. A fat, ugly
canary. And now you are a beautiful woman who fucks
Aristotle Onassis.
              Ari.
       This is how I talk. This is how I have always talked.
This is who I am. I'm coarse. I'm crude. I'm vulgar. Un-
like some people, I remember from whence I came.
       I remember. I remember too well.
       They listen to you sing this boring shit music and
clap and yell Brava! Brava la Divina! but what they all
want to know is what we do in bed. The two Greeks. The
two sweaty, piggy, beneath-us Greeks. The richest-man-
in-the-world Greek and the most-famous-singer-in-the-
world Greek. Together we rule the world. I have people
by the balls and I squeeze. I squeeze very hard and
without pity. I have you by the balls, Cecilia Sophia
Anna Maria Kalogeropoulou. Everyone is for sale and I
bought you.
       This part, "She sang Amina's great lament in a voice
suffused with tears."
       You give me class. I give you my big thick uncir-
cumcised Greek dick and you give me class. I give you
my wealth and you give me respect where I never had
any. I give you safety from your terror of the theatre, you
don't have to go there anymore. I give you everything you

want and need but love. I'm lucky. I don't need love. I
have class now. (*"He" laughs.*)
Everyone needs love, Ari. I'm proud, I'm very proud,
but when it comes to this, to love, to you, to us, I am not.
I don't give love to anyone but my children. Have a
child of mine and I will love him. Yes?
Yes, Ari.
Hey, canary, chin up. Look at me. You don't need
love either. You have theirs. The snobs and the fags. They
adore you. The snobs want to take you to dinner at Lutèce.
The fags just want to be you. Frankly, I'm not threatened.
You hate it when I call you canary, don't you? It's affec-
tionate. Can't you hear the affection in canary?
I was good tonight. I was very good.
Why don't you give all this up. It's *cacca*, *skata* anyway. Eh? You know it, I know it. You live on the boat.
You can go anywhere you want, stay as long as you want,
buy anything you want, within reason. Always within reason. I hate a woman who tries to bleed a man dry. Of
course she would have to be some woman to bleed this
motherfucker dry. Do you know how much I'm worth?
Do you have any idea of just how much money I have? I
breathe money, I sweat money, I shit money.
I don't have to sing anymore? I won't if you don't
want me.
Okay, so you don't sing anymore. You don't retire,
you stop. There's a difference. Retiring is depressing.
Stopping is class. They beg you. You're adamant. No
means no, you tell them. I bet you didn't know I had that
word in me, did you? Adamant. It means unshakable or
immovable, especially in opposition. Hard. Like diamonds. That's us, baby.
That's us, Ari. A matched pair.
But when I want you to sing, you sing. You sing only
for me. I have you under the most fucking exclusive con-

tract anybody ever had. And when I ask you to sing, you know what you're going to sing for me, baby? None of that opera *skata*. That song I taught you about the whore from Piraeus who took it five different ways at the same time. I had to tell you what four of those ways were.

I don't like that song, Ari.

Where have you been all your life, canary? Don't they fuck in the opera house?

I don't like that song.

Sing it anyway.

(*The aria proper has ended. We hear the audience applaud.*)

I never heard their applause here. I was too deep in a dream. Like Amina, I'd been sleepwalking. But there I was on the stage of La Scala. I was beautifully dressed, heavy with diamonds, real diamonds, my hair in a tight chignon bound with real white roses flown to Milan the day of the performance from the south of France. "The ghost of Maria Taglioni," one critic wrote. I was beautiful at last.

(*The music continues directly into the cabaletta conclusion of the scene and opera itself. We hear* MARIA*'s voice singing "Ah, non giunge."*)

I keep thinking of a pretty, slim blonde girl back at the conservatory in Athens. Madame de Hidalgo gave her the part of Amina at the student recital. I was so heartbroken but I wanted to scratch her face with my nails at the same time, too. I was cast as a nun in *Suor Angelica* instead. But I want to sing Amina in *Sonnambula*, Madame de Hidalgo. With your voice and figure you're better off as a nun, my child. Look at me now, Madame de Hidalgo. Listen to me now. Sometimes I think every performance I sing is for that pretty, slim blonde girl taking all those bows at the Conservatory. Whatever happened to her with her freshly laundered blouses and bags full of oranges? My sister was another slim pretty blonde. They're not up here, either one of them. I'm up here. The fat ugly greasy one with the thick glasses and bad skin is up here, and she's dressed by Piero Tosi and she's wearing so many diamonds she can scarcely move her arms and she is the absolute center of the universe right now.

I know they're all out there in the dark. My enemies. My mother. My sister. The other singers. Smiling. Waiting for me to fail. The dare-devil stuff is coming up. The hullabaloo. I'm not afraid. I welcome it. Reckless. You bet I'm reckless! Someone said I'd rather sing like Callas for one year than like anyone else for twenty!

Now the embellishments. The second time around. Never do it the same way twice. Flick your voice here. Lighten it. Shade it. Trill. Astonish.

(*She listens.*)

(*Slowly the rear of the stage will become the magnificent interior of La Scala.*)

Now the genius part of this production. Visconti has the house lights in the auditorium begin to come up while I'm still singing. Slowly, slowly. We're both waking up from a dream, the audience and me. The effect is unheard of. There's never been a night like this in the history of La Scala. The theatre is garlanded with fresh roses hung from the boxes. The audience is magnificently dressed. It's the biggest *prima* of the season. There's Tebaldi. There's Lollabrigida. Magnani. The Rainiers. They're all here. And here I am. Dead center-stage at the greatest theatre in Europe singing roulades in full voice. Hurling notes like thunderbolts. Daring anyone to challenge me. They can all see me but now I can see them. We are in the same room together at last. I have everyone where I want them.

They're not smiling now. With each phrase, I come closer to the footlights. The auditorium grows brighter and brighter as my voice goes higher and higher. People have stopped breathing. My revenge, my triumph are complete. The applause is washing over me. I only have one note left to sing. Ah, yes, it's over. I've won again!

(MARIA *stands listening to the ovation. It is tremendous. When it fades to silence, the lights have faded back up to the level of the master class. Both the* SOPRANO *and the* ACCOMPANIST *are waiting anxiously for her appraisal.*)

That was better.

SOPRANO: Thank you.

MARIA: Much better.

SOPRANO: Thank you.

MARIA: We'll take a break now.

(MARIA *goes to her chair, takes up her purse, and leaves the stage.*)

SOPRANO: Thank you.
I thought she was going to critique me.
(*To* ACCOMPANIST:) Now how do I make a graceful exit? They should teach us that. They should teach us a lot of things they don't.

ACCOMPANIST: Your score.

SOPRANO: Thank you.

(*He returns her score and they go off. The stage is bare except for the piano and* MARIA's *chair. The house lights are fully up now.*)

END OF ACT ONE

A C T   T W O

Someone has placed a bouquet of flowers on the piano.

The ACCOMPANIST *enters and sits quietly at the piano. This time he ignores the audience.*

The house lights are lowered. There is a long wait.

Eventually, MARIA *enters. She comes to the stage apron.*

MARIA: That's better. Eh? Isn't that better? With the lights like this? Eh? It's better we don't see you up here. That's how it is in the theatre. Just us and the music. Or that's how it should be. I know some singers, oh, yes, who look out at the audience, if you can imagine such a thing, when they're meant to be involved in a dramatic situation. Of course, I don't consider these people serious artists. *Pas du tout, n'est-ce que pas?* They're more like . . . oh, what's the word? . . . you know, help me: no arms or legs, they swim, throw them a fish and they—seals! That's what they are: performing seals! Excuse me?

(She cups her ear to hear someone in the audience.)

No. Absolutely not.

So. Where were we? Did you have a good interval? I had a friend, who shall remain nameless, who used to say his favorite part of opera was the intervals. Well, people like that, we're not going to concern ourselves with them today, thank God. To think there are actually people to whom beauty, art, what we do, isn't important! Don't get me wrong: I think we should be paid for what we do, and some of us are paid very well (it's no secret I was paid more than any of my rivals, which was the newspapers' word for them, not mine. As if I had any! How can you have rivals when no one else can do what you do?). So much has been written about it, so much nonsense. The point I'm making, and it's a very simple one, is that art is beauty and you should be paid for it. Am I making myself clear? Never give anything away. There's no more where it came from. We give the audience everything and when it's gone, *c'est ça, c'est tout. Basta, finito.* We're the ones who end up empty. "Ho dato tutto a te." Medea sings that to Jason when she learns he's abandoning her for another woman. A younger woman. A woman of importance. A princess. "Ho dato tutto a te." "I gave everything for you. Everything." That's what we artists do for people. Where would you be without us? Eh? Think about that. Just think about it while you're counting your millions or leading your boring lives with your boring wives.

(*To the* ACCOMPANIST:) Am I right?

ACCOMPANIST: I'm sorry?

MARIA: He knows I'm right.

    And the friend who shall remain nameless who preferred the intervals of *Norma* to *Norma* itself was no friend. I don't know the proper word for people who are everywhere in our lives but don't wish us well at all, as it turns out. Eh? Do you know what I'm talking about? She knows what I'm talking about. I know *one* word, but I think the ceiling would fall down if I used it in this holy

place, and I do believe we are in a holy place. The stage,
the theatre are sacred places, oh, yes. I lose my sense of
humor the moment I walk through the stage door. I'm
rambling. I had a terrible interval, actually. Well, you're
not interested in my problems. Any more than I'm interested in yours. We're here to work. Put everything else
behind us. Am I right?

ACCOMPANIST: Absolutely.

MARIA: Don't tell me . . . it's a Jewish name, I remember
that much . . . I remember the red sweater . . . *Po, po,
po!* . . . I give up.

ACCOMPANIST: Weinstock—Manny Weinstock.

MARIA: Of course it is! *Siete pronto, Signor Weinstock?*

ACCOMPANIST: *Sì.*

MARIA: *Bravo, bravo, arcibravo!* You're doing very well.

ACCOMPANIST: Thank you.

MARIA: Isn't he doing well? I salute you.

(*She applauds him.*)

We all salute you.

(*She encourages the audience to applaud him, then looks at
the index cards she has been carrying.*)

Who's next? Lady Macbeth, Tosca, Lucia. I must say,
what these students lack in voice and technique, they make
up for in self-confidence. Don't laugh. That's important.
Well, we shall see what we shall see. I wish them well.
Next victim! That was a joke. My last one, I promise.
        (*To the* ACCOMPANIST:) And what is that folderol on
the piano there, please?

ACCOMPANIST: You mean the flowers? They're for you. You have an unknown admirer. Very operatic.

MARIA: Is this a classroom or a circus?

(ANOTHER SOPRANO *is coming out onto the stage. She is in an evening gown.*)

That was very naughty of someone. I won't pretend I'm not flattered, but I'm also not amused. Very, very naughty. (*To the* SOPRANO:) *Avanti, avanti!* Don't linger. If you're going to enter, enter. If you don't want to be out here, go away. Don't giggle out there. Don't mind them, dear, I'll be right with you. Are you going somewhere after this?

SOPRANO: No.

MARIA (*reading the card that accompanied the flowers*): "Brava, La Divina. We love you." "La Divina." Don't make me laugh. And it's always "We love you," never "*I* love you." So. Now who have we here?

SOPRANO: Sharon Graham.

MARIA: Sharon Graham. Definitely not Greek.

SOPRANO: No.

MARIA: What's in a name, eh? I was Maria Meneghini Callas for a time. Of course, I was Signora Meneghini for a time as well. So. Sharon Graham. What are you going to sing for us?

SOPRANO: Lady Macbeth?

MARIA: Are you sure you want to do that, Sharon?

SOPRANO: I also have Queen of the Night, "Der Hölle Rache" and Norma, the "Casta diva."

MARIA: I think we'll stay with Lady Macbeth. The Sleepwalking Scene, I suppose.

SOPRANO: No, "Vieni! t'affretta," I thought.

MARIA: Ah, the Letter Scene! Well, that's something. They usually all want to start with the Sleepwalking Scene. You're humble, like me, that's good. So. This is her entrance aria, yes?

SOPRANO: Yes.

MARIA: So what are you doing out here? Go away. We don't want to see you yet.

SOPRANO: You want me to go off and come back out?

MARIA: No, I want you to enter. You're on a stage. Use it. Own it. This is opera, not a voice recital. Anyone can stand there and sing. An artist enters and *is*.

SOPRANO: I thought this was a classroom.

MARIA: It doesn't matter. Never miss an opportunity to theatricalize. Astonish us, Sharon.

SOPRANO: How do I do that?

MARIA: You can start by not entering as Sharon Graham. Enter as Lady Macbeth. Enter as Shakespeare's Lady Macbeth. Enter as Verdi's Lady Macbeth.

SOPRANO: I'll do my best.

MARIA: And Sharon, may I say one more thing? That's a beautiful gown, obviously. We've all been admiring it. It's gorgeous. I wish I had one like it.

SOPRANO: Thank you.

MARIA: But don't ever wear anything like that before midnight at the earliest, and certainly not to class. We're talking about what's appropriate. This is a master class, not some Cinderella's ball. Eh? Off you go now. And come back as her. Come back as Lady.

(*The* SOPRANO *exits.*)

Sometimes we just have to say these things, eh? Am I right? I learned the hard way. I didn't have anyone to tell me these things. I auditioned for Edward Johnson at the old Met wearing a red-and-white polka-dot dress, white gloves, a blue hat with a veil, and what I later learned were known as Joan Crawford "catch me/your-F-word me" pumps. I'm sorry, but that's what they were called. I was overweight and looked like an American flag singing *Madama Butterfly*. No wonder I wasn't engaged. She'll thank me one day.

Are we ready?

(*The* ACCOMPANIST *nods.*)

I haven't heard this music in years. Even the thought of it makes the hairs on the back of my head stand out.
I guess I'm ready. Begin.

(*The* ACCOMPANIST *begins to play the introduction to Lady Macbeth's entrance aria.* MARIA *listens hard, making sounds along with it, rather than actually singing the notes.*)

Satanic music, don't you think? We know where this music is coming from, don't we? What part of her body? Verdi knew his Shakespeare. The curtain is flying up now. No Sharon yet. This is an interesting choice for an entrance. I was onstage at this point.

(*The music stops. No sign of the* SOPRANO.)

Sharon? We're all waiting. (*To the audience:*) Excuse me.

(*She leaves the stage and comes back a moment later.*)

No Sharon. She's gone. If her skin is that thin, she's not suited for this career. It's not like I said anything about her voice. I didn't even let her open her mouth. This will make the papers. They'll have a fine time with this. "Callas Hurts Student's Feelings."

This is just what I was talking about: If you're going to stand up here, naked, and let people judge you, you can't afford to have feelings like Sharon's. A performance is a struggle. You have to win. The audience is the enemy. We have to bring you to your knees because we're right. If I'm worried about what you're thinking about me, I can't win. I beg, I cringe for your favor instead. "Ho dato tutto a te." Eh? It doesn't work that way. You have to make them beg for yours. Dominate them. "Ho dato tutto a te." Eh? Art is domination. It's making people think that for that precise moment in time there is only one way, one voice. Yours. Eh? Anyone's feelings can be hurt. Only an artist can say "Ho dato tutto a te" center stage at La Scala and even Leonard Bernstein forgets he's Leonard Bernstein and listens to you.

Next student, please. Is there water? I need water.

ACCOMPANIST: Right over there. Please, let me.

MARIA: There's one advantage in being this nearsighted. You don't have to follow the conductor. How can you? You can't see him. But I never made them follow me. No, we worked together. *Insieme. Tutto insieme.* Art is collaboration, too. Domination. Collaboration. *Ecco.* If you have feelings like Sharon, hide them. It's that simple. That's what I did. Excuse me.

(*She drinks as the* TENOR *comes out onto the stage.*)

Avanti, avanti. You all lack presence. Look at me. I'm drinking water and I have presence. Stand straight. Let us see who you are. *Bravo!* You're a good-looking man. You have what the Italians call *bella figura.*

TENOR: Thank you.

MARIA: That wasn't a compliment. It was a statement. We're talking turkey here. A singer has to know his assets. This is a business too, after all, let's never forget that. Domination. Collaboration. Assets. What are you?

TENOR: You mean my name?

MARIA: No, I mean your voice.

TENOR: I'm a tenor. Couldn't you tell?

MARIA: A tenor. *Gran Dio.* God save us sopranos from you tenors. And that is the only tenor joke you're going to hear from me.

TENOR: People think we're stupid.

MARIA: I wonder why that is.

TENOR: I don't know.

MARIA: Actually, I love tenors. When they sing, it's our chance to go to our dressing rooms and catch our breath. But no such luck today. I'll be right over here. Are you nervous?

TENOR: No.

MARIA: Good. What's your name?

TENOR: Tony.

MARIA: Tony? Just Tony?

TENOR: You mean when I sing! Anthony Candolino.

MARIA: I always mean when you sing. I only mean when you sing. This is a master class, not a psychiatrist's office. Are any of you out there undergoing psychiatry? I hope not.

Tell us about yourself. Your training. Your professional experience, if any. Your hopes, your dreams.

TENOR: I have a BA in music from USC and an MFA in voice from UCLA.

MARIA: Go on.

TENOR: I've done Billy Jackrabbit in *Fanciulla del West* with Opera Ohio and I'm covering Rinuccio in *Gianni Schicchi* for Opera West.

MARIA: We all have to begin somewhere. You haven't told us about your dreams.

TENOR: I want to be a great singer. Like you. I want to be rich and famous. Like you. I want it all. Like you. Move over, Richard Tucker. Here comes Tony Candolino.

MARIA: May I have more water, please?

(There is a longish pause.)

TENOR: Are we waiting for your water?

MARIA: No, we're waiting for you.

TENOR: I've chosen *Tosca.*

(The STAGEHAND *enters with another pitcher of water.)*

Cavaradossi's aria, the first act.

MARIA: I can tell you right now: if you hold the B-flat longer than the composer asks for, it's going to be off with your extremely handsome head.
      (To the STAGEHAND:*)* Thank you.
      (To the TENOR:*)* No showing off, eh?

TENOR: I'll be happy if I get the B-flat, period.

MARIA: No happier than we.

STAGEHAND: You're welcome.

(*He exits.*)

(*The* ACCOMPANIST *begins to play the introduction to "Recondita armonia" from Puccini's* Tosca.)

> Just a moment, Tony. Feelings like Sharon's: we use them, we don't give them away on some voodoo witch doctor's couch. Again.

(*The* ACCOMPANIST *plays; the* TENOR *begins to sing.*)

TENOR: "Dammi i colori."

MARIA: I'm going to stop you.

TENOR: I got more out than the soprano did. You stopped her at "Oh."

MARIA: This is no joke. I don't know why you're smiling.

TENOR: I wasn't smiling.

MARIA: Was he smiling?

TENOR: I'm sorry.

MARIA: You're either going to flirt with the public or we're going to work. Which is it going to be?

TENOR: Work.

MARIA: Now what were you doing?

TENOR: Nothing. I was singing.

MARIA: You were right the first time. You were *just* singing, which equals nothing. Again.

(*The* ACCOMPANIST *begins again.*)

TENOR (*singing*): "Dammi i colori."

MARIA: Where are you?

TENOR: You mean right now? Or in the opera?

MARIA: No games, Tony.

TENOR: I'm in Rome, I'm in a church, I'm painting a picture. I just asked the old Sacristan for my paints. That's what "Dammi i colori" means: "Give me the paints."

MARIA: What church? Whose picture? Quick, quick. I don't have all day.

TENOR: I don't know. St. Patrick's! No, that's in. St. Peter's? St. Somebody's! Whose portrait? Some woman's obviously. Tosca's? No. The Mona Lisa, I don't know!

MARIA: So, let me get this straight. You don't know where you are, you are about to paint a portrait but you don't know of whom, and yet you are about to sing an aria. No wonder people don't like opera.

TENOR: I don't think you have to know all those things. I have a voice, I have a technique, I even have a B-flat.

MARIA: So do I. It's not enough.

TENOR: It was for Mario Lanza. I'm sorry. I love Mario Lanza. He's my hero. So kill me.

MARIA: You haven't done your homework, Tony.

TENOR: I just came out here to sing for you.

MARIA: I'm not interested in just singing.

TENOR: Sing and get your feedback.

MARIA: My what? My "feedback"? What an ugly word. What is feedback? He wants my feedback. I don't give feedback.

TENOR: Your response.

MARIA: I respond to what I feel. I feel nothing but anger for someone who so little treasures his art. You're not prepared, Mr. Tony Tight Pants. Go home. You're wasting our time. Next student.

TENOR: No.

MARIA: No?

TENOR: No.

MARIA: That's the first interesting thing you've said since you came out here.

TENOR: I came here to sing.

MARIA: You weren't ready.

TENOR: I'm going to sing.

MARIA: And I can't stop you?

TENOR: I need your help. I want to sing. I want to sing well. I know I have a voice and I know it's not enough. I want to be an artist.
(*He sings:*) "Dammi i colori."
(*To* MARIA:) Please.

(MARIA *nods to the* ACCOMPANIST, *who begins again.*)

MARIA: You're in the church of Sant' Andrea della Valle, just off the Corso. Do you know Rome?

TENOR: No.

MARIA: It doesn't matter. It's ten a.m. on a beautiful spring morning. You made love all night to Floria Tosca, the most beautiful woman in Rome. And now you're painting another woman, unobserved, as she prays to the Blessed Mother. They're both beautiful, but it's Tosca's body against yours you feel. Now sing.

TENOR: It doesn't say anything about ten a.m. or spring or Tosca's body in the score.

MARIA: It should say it in your imagination. Otherwise you have notes, nothing but notes. Sing!

TENOR: "Recondita armonia."

MARIA: On the breath, on the breath!

TENOR: "di bellezze diverse!"

MARIA: Don't force.

TENOR: "È bruna Floria."

MARIA: Much better.

TENOR: "l'ardente amante mia."

MARIA: You're singing about your mistress! Look happy.

ACCOMPANIST: "Scherza coi fanti e lascia stare i santi!"

TENOR: *Bravo!*

MARIA: Concentrate.

TENOR:

"E te, beltade ignota,
cinta di chiome bionde,
tu azzurro hai l'occhio,
Tosca ha l'occhio nero."

MARIA (*at will, during the above*): That's right, open it up. Let me feel that blond hair. Blue eyes. Tosca's black eyes now.

ACCOMPANIST: "Scherza coi fanti e lascia stare i santi!"

MARIA (*as before*): Do you know what you're singing about, Tony?

(He shakes his head while continuing to sing.)

Art, in all its mystery, blends these different beauties together. One woman, one ideal!

TENOR:

"L'arte nel suo mistero
le diverse bellezze insiem confonde:"

MARIA: Here it comes. The Big Tune! Go for it!

TENOR:

"ma, nel ritrar costei . . .
il mio solo pensiero,
ah! il mio sol pensier sei tu,
Tosca, sei tu!"

(MARIA *silently mouths the final high notes along with the* TENOR.)

(The music ends. MARIA *is silent.)*

MARIA: That was beautiful. I have nothing more to say. That was beautiful.

TENOR: I've also prepared *Werther* and "Ah, sì, ben mio."

MARIA: That won't be necessary. Are we scheduled for a break now? No? Great music always takes so much out of me. I feel quite faint. That will be all, Mr. Candoloro.

TENOR: You can call me Tony.

MARIA: I wish you well on your career.

TENOR: Thank you. Don't you have any advice for me?

MARIA: Remember the springtime. Now go.

(He goes. MARIA *sits in the chair.)*

MARIA: Next student. I never really listened to that aria. I'm quite emotional. I was always backstage preparing for my entrance. "Mario, Mario"—just two words from offstage and your goose is cooked. I've seen entire audiences turn against a Tosca because they didn't like the way she sang "Mario, Mario." It's a terrible career, actually. I don't know why I bothered. I didn't say that. You didn't hear it and I didn't say it!

(*The* SOPRANO *comes back onto the stage.*)

SOPRANO: I'm back!

(MARIA *looks at her blankly.*)

I'd like to try again. I've been in the ladies' room throwing up. I must have eaten something.

(MARIA *holds up her hand to stop her from going into further detail.*)

So should I go out and come in again?

(MARIA *nods.*)

I'll yell when I'm ready.

(*The* ACCOMPANIST *nods.* SOPRANO *exits.*)

MARIA: Water. I need more water.

SOPRANO (*offstage*): I'm ready!

(*The* ACCOMPANIST *begins Lady Macbeth's entrance music yet again.* SOPRANO *enters at the appropriate moment. The music stops. She begins.*)

SOPRANO (*reciting*): " 'Nel dì della vittoria io le incontrai. Stupito io n'era per le udite cose;' "

MARIA: Where's your letter? You're meant to be reading a letter.

SOPRANO: I was pretending to hold one. Couldn't you tell?

MARIA: I don't want pretending. You're not good enough. I want truth. This is a letter.

(*She seizes a piece of paper and thrusts it at* SOPRANO.)

What are you saying?

SOPRANO: I'm saying, " 'I met them on the day of victory. I was rapt in wonder at the things I heard. When the King's messengers hailed me as Thane of Cawdor.' "

MARIA: Put some wonder in your voice! Thane of Cawdor! It's what she's dreamed of.

SOPRANO: " 'Thane of Cawdor! A prediction made by those same seers who foretold a crown upon my head. Keep deep in your heart these secrets. Addio.' "

MARIA: Do you know this speech in Shakespeare?

SOPRANO: I've read the play, of course, but that was in high school.

MARIA: You want to sing this music without knowing your Shakespeare!

SOPRANO: I'm not an actress. I'm just a singer.

MARIA: Do you think Verdi composed it without knowing his Shakespeare? *Vergogna*, Sharon, shame. And that wasn't an entrance. You came on, but it wasn't an entrance. That goes for all of you, too. An entrance is everything. It's how we present ourselves to an audience. It's how we present ourselves in life. A man who would barge in on a woman in her bath is a pig. She should know from his entrance how it's going to end. I'll show you an entrance. You can set the scene for our colleagues. Just read from the score.

(*She quickly leaves the stage. The* SOPRANO *is all at sea. She sits cautiously on the edge of* MARIA*'s chair. She picks up and reads from* MARIA*'s score.*)

MARIA (*offstage*): *Sto pronta, maestro!*

(*The* ACCOMPANIST *begins again.*)

SOPRANO: "Scene Two. The grand hall in Macbeth's castle. There are several rooms leading off it. There is a grand staircase descending from the floor above. There are two small thrones. It is night. A violent storm is raging. Thunder. Lightning. Rain. Curtain. Lady Macbeth enters at the top of the stairs. She is magnificently arrayed. She is reading a letter. Her manner is agitated, her expression fierce. She comes down to the footlights and, in the silence, speaks."

(MARIA *has entered as Verdi's Lady Macbeth, reading a letter.*)

MARIA: " 'Nel dì della vittoria io le incontrai.
Stupito io n'era per le udite cose;
Quando i nunzi del Re me salutaro
Sir di Caudore.
Vaticinio uscito dalle veggenti stesse che
predissero un serto al capo mio. Racchiudi in cor
questo segreto. Addio.' "

(MARIA *begins to sing the first lines of Lady Macbeth's recitative. What comes out is a cracked and broken thing. A voice in ruins.*

It is a terrible moment.)

"Ambizioso spirto tu sei, Macbetto . . ." Go on, you're the student here. Not I. And see how important a prop is?

SOPRANO: You hardly looked at the letter.

MARIA: She has it memorized. She's read it over and over and over. My choice. Not Verdi's. Not Shakespeare's. Callas. You think you can do that now?

SOPRANO: Not like you.

MARIA: I don't want it done like me. I want it done like Verdi.

ACCOMPANIST: With music?

MARIA: Yes, with music. This isn't a play.

(*The* ACCOMPANIST *begins to play and* SOPRANO *to recite as* MARIA *coaches, cajoles.*)

SOPRANO: "Ambizioso spirto tu sei, Macbetto."

MARIA: There's two *t*'s in "Macbetto." I want to hear them.

SOPRANO: "Mac—"

MARIA: Don't repeat, keep going!

SOPRANO: "Alla grandezza aneli, ma sarai tu malvagio?"

MARIA: "You would be great, but will you be wicked?" Ah, there's the question! Don't stop, don't stop!

SOPRANO: "Pien di misfatti è il calle della potenza e mal per lui che il piede dubitoso vi pone, e retrocede!"

MARIA: He's weak. She knows it. She must be strong for both of them!

SOPRANO: The aria?

MARIA: Yes, don't even think of stopping! You are Lady Macbeth!

(*The* ACCOMPANIST *goes directly into the introduction to the aria proper as* MARIA *circles the* SOPRANO, *working with her.*)

Use this introduction to focus yourself. Why are you moving your hand? Never move your hand unless you follow it with your heart and soul.

SOPRANO: How do I know when to move it at all?

MARIA: The composer tells you. It's all in the music. Now!

SOPRANO: "Vieni! t'affretta! accendere."

MARIA: Bite into those words. Spit them out.

SOPRANO: "Ti vo' quel freddo core!"

MARIA: Let yourself go. Who are you saving it for?

SOPRANO:

"L'audace impresa a compiere
Io ti darò valore;"

MARIA: She's going to give him some balls. I'm sorry, but that's what she's saying.

SOPRANO: "Di Scozia a te promettono"

MARIA: The melody broadens here. Let it through you.

SOPRANO: "Le profetesse il trono."

MARIA: The throne of Scotland has been promised to him! What is he waiting for?

SOPRANO:

"Che tardi? Accetta il dono,
Ascendivi a regnar.
Ascendivi a regnar,
Accetta, accetta il dono . . ."

MARIA: This is important to you! You make me want to shake you, Sharon!

SOPRANO:

"Ascendivi a regnar.
Che tardi?"

MARIA: What are you waiting for? Accept the gift. Take what
I'm giving you.

SOPRANO:

"Che tardi?
Accetta il dono,
Ascendi, ascendi, ascendivi a regnar."

MARIA: Rise and rule. Rise and take your place in this
world.

SOPRANO:

"Che tardi? Accetta il dono,
ascendivi a regnar.
Che tardi? Accetta il dono,
ascendivi a regnar.
Che tardi? Che tardi?"

MARIA: This isn't just an opera. This is your life.

SOPRANO:

"Ah! . . .
ascendivi a regnar."

(*The music for the aria proper ends.*)

MARIA: Go on.

SOPRANO: The cabaletta?

MARIA: Yes, the cabaletta! Why do you want to keep stopping?
This is where everything changes. The dramatic situation,
the tempo. An aria without its cabaletta is like sex without
an orgasm. I don't mean to speak crudely, but sometimes

even we artists must sink to the gutter to rise to the stars.
Eh? Am I right?
So what happens here? Hurry up, you're running out
of steam.

SOPRANO: Someone comes in and.

MARIA: Not someone. No one is someone.

SOPRANO: A servant.

MARIA: Now you're talking!

SOPRANO: He tells her that the king, Duncan, will be at their
castle that very evening.

MARIA: Is Macbeth with him?

SOPRANO: Yes!

MARIA: And how does that make her feel?

SOPRANO: Happy?

MARIA: Don't keep looking at me for answers, Sharon. Tell me,
show me. *Vite, vite!*

SOPRANO: Really happy.

MARIA: Love happy? Christmas-morning happy?

SOPRANO: Murder happy!

MARIA: Ah! And what is she going to do about it?

SOPRANO: She's going to sing a cabaletta!

MARIA: She's going to kill the king! Do you know what that
means?

SOPRANO: Yes, it's terrible.

MARIA: Not to her! Do you believe women can have balls,
Sharon?

SOPRANO: Some women. Yes, I do!

MARIA: Verdi is daring you to show us yours, Sharon. Will you do it?

SOPRANO: Yes!

MARIA: *Andiamo.*

(*The* ACCOMPANIST *goes into the music accompanying the bridge between the aria and the cabaletta.* MARIA *"becomes" the Servant who brings Lady Macbeth the news of King Duncan's arrival.*)

MARIA: The music here is ridiculous. Ignore it.

ACCOMPANIST: "Al cader della sera il Re qui giunge."

SOPRANO: "Che di? Macbetto è seco?"

ACCOMPANIST: "Ei l'accompagna. La nuova, o donna, è certa."

SOPRANO: "Trovi accoglienza, quale un Re si merta."

MARIA: Wait till he's gone. Keep the mask on. It's hard. This is what you've been waiting for. Go!

SOPRANO: "Duncano."

MARIA: Use the words. "Duncano."

SOPRANO: I'm sorry.

MARIA: Haste makes waste. Again, please, Sharon.

(*She glances at her wristwatch.*)

SOPRANO: "Duncano sarà qui . . ."

MARIA: She can't believe her ears.

SOPRANO: "Qui . . ."

MARIA: When? How soon? Before you burst with it.

SOPRANO: "Qui la notte?"

MARIA: Tonight! It's now or never. She's going crazy here. It's all in the music. Listen to those dissonances. Don't act, listen. It's always in the music, Sharon. Don't look at me for help. Listen to Verdi, listen to Shakespeare.

SOPRANO:

"Or tutti sorgete,
Ministri infernali,
Che al sangue incorate,
Spingete i mortali!
Tu, notte, ne avvolgi
Di tenebra immota"

MARIA: Is there anything you would kill for, Sharon?

SOPRANO: I don't think so.

MARIA: A man, a career?

SOPRANO: Not off the top of my head.

MARIA: You have to listen to something in yourself to sing this difficult music. When I sang Medea I could feel the stones of Epidaurus beneath the wooden floorboards at La Scala. I was standing where Medea, Electra, Clytemnestra had stood. There was a direct line through me to the composer to Euripides to Medea herself. These people really existed. Medea, Lady Macbeth. Or don't you believe that? Eh? This is all make-believe to you?

SOPRANO: I've never really thought about it.

MARIA: That's because you're young. You will. In time. Know how much suffering there can be in store for a woman.

SOPRANO: But you were young when you first sang Lady Macbeth and Medea.

MARIA: I was never young. I couldn't afford to be. Not to get to where I was going. Anyway. Enough of that. You came back. You had *Mut*. That's something. Do you know that German word? It means courage. I had to know it when I sang *Fidelio* for the Germans during the Occupation during the war. It was at the Theatre Herod Atticus in Athens. I was eighteen years old. I needed lots of *Mut* that day. *Mut!* It's a good word, don't you think? *Mut*. I don't like many things German, but I like *Mut*. Again.

SOPRANO: You want me to do it again?

MARIA: Yes! Off you go now. And this is for all of you: there are no short cuts in art, no easy ways. This isn't life, where there are so many. There is no being at center stage as if by magic. There is always an entrance first, just as there is always an exit after. Art is about those transitions. There is only discipline, technique and *Mut*. The rest is kaka-peepee-doodoo. I'm sorry, but there it is. Eh?

(She listens to someone in the audience.)

I was asked something about genius, inspiration. Well, of course. Without them, we're nothing. We're a Milanov at best. Don't snicker. It was a great voice, but an artist? I don't think so.

    Are you ready back there?

    (To the ACCOMPANIST:*)* What is her name?

ACCOMPANIST: Sharon.

MARIA: Are you ready back there, Sharon?

SOPRANO *(offstage)*: I think so.

MARIA: Don't think, don't hope, do. *Mut*, Sharon, *Mut*. Every eye is on you.

    (To the audience:) Notice I didn't say "ear."

(*To the* SOPRANO:) All right, Sharon. I'm not going
to interrupt this time.

(*To the* ACCOMPANIST:) *Per piacere, Maestro Manny.*

(*The* ACCOMPANIST *begins the introduction to Lady Macbeth's
entrance aria.*)

Does anyone know what time it is? I have a beauty parlor
appointment after this. I can't get a good wash and set in
this city. Ssshh! You can tell me later. *Eccola!*

(*The* SOPRANO *enters with a prop letter and begins the scene
again. It isn't long before* MARIA *is reciting the words along
with her.*)

MARIA: Ah, ah! Careful! That's better. Don't look at me. You're
on your own now.

MARIA and SOPRANO: " 'Nel dì della vittoria io le incontrai . . .
Stupito io n'era per le udite cose;
Quando i nunzi del Re mi salutaro
Sir di Caudore; vaticinio uscito
Dalle veggenti stesse
Che predissero un serto al capo mio.
Racchiudi in cor questo segreto. Addio.' "

SOPRANO: "Ambizioso spirto
Tu sei, Macbetto. . . .
Alla grandezza aneli
Ma sarai tu malvagio?"

(*The* SOPRANO *continues, but we no longer hear her. Instead,
there is a light change. This time we hear an orchestra playing
the turbulent introduction to Lady Macbeth's "Letter Scene."
It is a live performance from 1952.*)

MARIA: This infernal music. Come, fill me with your malevo-
lence. Let me be her. That sound of the curtain parting.
The stage dust. Don't breathe it in. They see me. "Who

is this fat Greek girl we never heard of making her debut in our temple of temples?'' Ah! The silence. It's time. Begin.

(*This time* MARIA *reads the letter along with her own voice on the recording.*)

MARIA & RECORDING: '' 'Nel dì della vittoria io le incontrai . . .
Stupito io n'era per le udite cose;
Quando i nunzi del Re me salutaro
Sir di Caudore; vaticinio uscito
Dalle veggenti stesse
Che predissero un serto al capo mio.
Racchiudi in cor questo segreto. Addio.' ''

MARIA: They're waiting for you to sing.

RECORDING: ''Ambizioso spirto
Tu sei, Macbetto . . .''

MARIA: That's who I am! This voice.

RECORDING: ''Alla grandezza aneli,
Ma sarai tu malvagio?''

MARIA: Yes, I dare to go to the greatest heights! My whole life has led up to this moment.

RECORDING: ''Pien di misfatti è il calle
Della potenza, e mal per lui che il piede
Dubitoso vi pone, e retrocede!''

MARIA: A debut at La Scala. With Maestro De Sabata, no less. Good chest note there. Now the first high C. They're impressed. Just wait. You haven't heard anything yet.

(*The orchestra plays the introduction to the aria proper.*)

Ah, Verdi! Ah, Shakespeare! Ah, my own ambition!

(The aria itself has begun now. During the following, MARIA *will occasionally listen to it, comment on it, but will sometimes not even be aware of it.)*

The costume is so heavy. I can scarcely move. They've made me look so fat.

"But the *signorina* is, how shall we say? Ample. There are limits to what we can do. We're not magicians." Hideous giggling behind little fairy hands.

The *signorina* is Signora Meneghini, my wife, and you will show her courtesy and respect and you will make her another costume and send me the bill.

Thank you, Battista.

You are my wife, Maria. I adore you.

I can breathe now. Maybe I'll have a success now!

He's old enough to be her father.

With a figure like that, who else would want her? She should count her blessings.

But that voice!

You can't fuck a voice.

I know what they're saying. I don't care. I know what I want and after tonight I'll have it. They haven't heard anything like this since Malibran! In less than one year I've become the Queen of La Scala. That has to count for something. La Divina. Imagine being called La Divina. I am La Divina. Listen to that! I've won, Battista, I've made something of myself.

Why can't you say you love me, Maria?

Don't ask me that. Not now. I have a performance. Where is my eyebrow pencil? Someone's taken it. They're all jealous. They want to see me fail. They take my makeup. They tear my costumes. Where is my rouge? Everything is in disarray. Not now, Battista. I can't bear to see you in my dressing room mirror standing there behind me, always asking me if I love you. You got what you wanted. A famous wife. I got what I wanted. This night and every night that I go out there and sing. When I sing, I'm not fat. I'm not ugly. I'm not an old man's wife. I'm Callas. I'm La Divina. I'm everything I wanted to be. So don't bring up love when you look at me in my mirror like that, Battista. Love can wait.

Tell me, is the theatre full? Has the tenor apologized? He called me a cow. Have you paid the claque, Battista? We have work to do, my husband. Lady Macbeth, Norma, Lucia, Tosca. We have made as unholy a pact as Macbeth and his Lady. I've become thin. Look at me. Another Audrey Hepburn, they're all saying. I've become a beautiful woman, Battista. I like being beautiful. I had thirty-seven curtain calls at the theatre tonight. They say a student leapt from the balcony for love of me, but he wasn't killed. "Then he didn't really love me," I told the reporters, and I laughed for the photographers. I laughed! I can't bear it when you look at me like that. It's worse here, when we're alone, than at the theatre. I want you to sleep in your room. You're an old man. The thought of sleeping with you repulses me.

Wait! And yet I do love you. Not the way you hoped, I know. Not the way I hoped, either. I thought it would suffice. Why are you looking at me like that? You know what I'm going to say. It's been in all the papers. Of course he's going to marry me. I'm sorry, Battista. I never meant you harm.

I told him, Ari. I think I broke his heart. We must be very happy together, you and I, to have caused so much pain. I realize now: all those years of singing, perfecting my voice, so that it would express everything I felt, they were for you. My song of love was for you, Ari, all those great passionate melodies, Bellini, Verdi, Donizetti, my siren songs to a man who doesn't even like opera! It's very funny when you think about it. A great ballerina dancing for a blind man. I am so happy! This moment is why I was born. I have news, Ari, such great and wonderful news. I'm going to have your child. No, *our* child, our son. I would not insult you by giving you a daughter. And we will name him Odysseus for the greatest Greek hero of them all, like you, and because he wandered the world the longest, like me, until he came home to love.

No, I don't need your child to feel like a woman. I am a woman. I don't need anything. Some people would say I don't need you. I want a child. Your child. I love you. There, I've said it. Don't ask me to do that. Why would you ask me to do that? What do you mean, you've changed your mind? I'm not a young woman. This may be my only chance. I'll give up anything, my career even, everything I've worked for, but not this. Then don't marry me. I won't do it. You can't make me. I won't let you make me! Don't leave me! I've been alone all my life until now!

O child I will never see or know or nurse or say how much I love you, forgive me.

It's done, Ari.

Now what?

Sing? You're telling me to sing? Sing what? "Stormy Weather"? Sing where? In the street? I'm losing my voice! Don't you read the papers? I'm getting by on sheer nerve. I always did. That's what's going, not the voice.

They fired me at La Scala. At my last performance, in the final scene, I went right to the stage apron, just meters from where the general manager was sitting in his box, the same man who had said my services in his theatre were no longer necessary, and I pointed right at him and I sang "Il palco funesto!" I thought I was losing my mind, not Imogene. The audience gasped. Ghiringhelli reeled from the force of it. But it wasn't him I was speaking to. It was you. "Il palco funesto!" "The fatal scaffold!"

They say it was the greatest ovation in the history of La
Scala. He ordered them to ring down the fire curtain to
stop my applause.

(*She kneels.*)

Marry me, Ari. Your canary is asking you to marry her.

(*She opens her arms.*)

"Ho dato tutto a te."

(*The* Macbeth *aria is over. We hear the audience applauding.*)

SOPRANO: Madame Callas?

MARIA: Ssshh! Listen, they're applauding. Never move on your
applause. It shortens it.

SOPRANO: No one was applauding. You told them not to.

MARIA: I would never tell anyone that, *ma chère*. The worst
part about being a teacher is being misunderstood. Applause is what we live on. Sometimes it's the only thing
we have. Did that feel better that time, yes?

SOPRANO: I don't know. What do you think?

MARIA: I think you have a lovely voice.

SOPRANO: Thank you.

MARIA: I think you have some spirit, too.

SOPRANO: Thank you.

MARIA: I wish you well.

SOPRANO: Thank you.

MARIA: But I think you should work on something more appropriate for your limitations. Mimi or Micaëla maybe.
But Lady Macbeth, Norma. I don't think so. These roles

require something else. Something. How shall I say this? Something special. Something that can't be taught or passed on or copied or even talked about. Genius. Inspiration. A gift of God. Some recompense for everything else.

(*The* SOPRANO *bursts into tears.*)

What did I say? This is what I'm talking about. *Mut! Coraggio!* It takes more than a pretty voice to build a career.

SOPRANO: I wish I'd never done this. I don't like you. You can't sing anymore and you're envious of anyone younger who can. You just want us to sing like you, recklessly, and lose our voices in ten years like you did. Well, I won't do it. I don't want to. I don't want to sing like you. I hate people like you. You want to make the world dangerous for everyone just because it was for you.

(*She leaves. There is an awkward silence.*)

MARIA: So. *Po, po, po.* I think we should stop here. Miss Graham thought I wanted her to sing like Maria Callas. No one can sing like Maria Callas. Only Cecilia Sophia Anna Maria Kalogeropoulou could sing like Maria Callas. I'm very upset. I'm hurt. As strange as it may seem to some of you, I have feelings, too. Anyway. That's another story. Et cetera, et cetera, eh? Maybe this whole business of teaching is a mistake.

If I have seemed harsh, it is because I have been harsh with myself. I'm not good with words, but I have tried to reach you. To communicate something of what I feel about what we do as artists, as musicians and as human beings. The sun will not fall down from the sky if there are no more *Traviata*s. The world can and will go on without us but I have to think that we have made this world a better place. That we have left it richer, wiser than had we not chosen the way of art. The older I get, the less I know, but I am certain that what we do matters. If I didn't believe that.

You must know what you want to do in life, you must decide, for we cannot do everything. Do not think singing is an easy career. It is a lifetime's work; it does not stop here. Whether I continue singing or not doesn't matter. Besides, it's all there in the recordings. What matters is that you use whatever you have learned wisely. Think of the expression of the words, of good diction, and of your own deep feelings. The only thanks I ask is that you sing properly and honestly. If you do this, I will feel repaid.

Well, that's that.

(*She gathers her things and goes. The* ACCOMPANIST *closes the lid on the piano. He takes the bouquet someone left there and follows after her. The stage is bare. The house lights are turned up.*)

THE END